A FIRE in the SHADOWS

Mona Banerjee

INDIA • SINGAPORE • MALAYSIA

ISBN 979-8-89544-296-8

Contents

ONE LAST TIME

Wind of my soul,
Fill the sails of this old boat
And push it out on the sea of life
One last time.
Tear the frayed ropes,
Raise the rusty anchor
And let it ride free and wild
One last time.
Too long has it been moored,
Resting in still waters,
Dreaming of what might have been.
The time has come
To face the storm,
To rip apart the tangled nets
And breast the waves
Or sink beneath their flying spume.
Wind of my soul,
I need you now
To fill these tattered sails
And set me free
One last time.

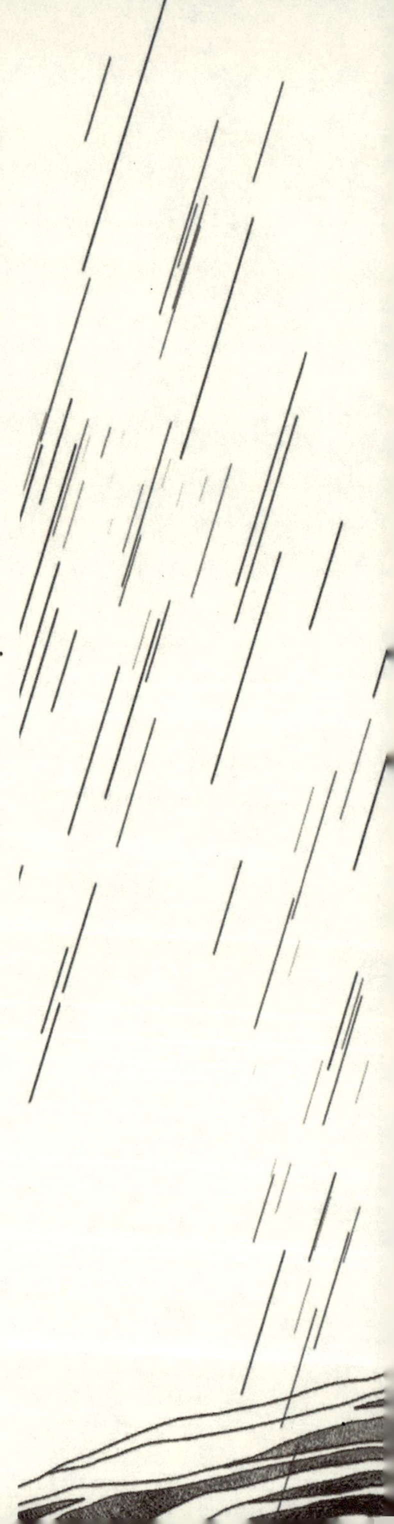

FIRE IN THE SHADOWS

Fire in the shadows
Licking at the dust of ages,
Cringing from cobwebs that glue the mind,
And distorted images that peep and leer.
But they can't douse
The fire in the shadows.

It's waiting for that one breath of air,
Blowing from its own heart,
Stirring cobwebs, weakening clammy links.
Breath that stirs the dust with its releasing finger.
Piercing the darkness, showing the way…

And the fire in the shadows creeps out.
Slowly at first, reaching fingers of light
Out of the shadows.
Then it takes life from its own breath
To blaze, to light and burn, and warm and scare
And show the way.

Fire in the shadows, free …
Free to leap up and touch the heavens
And be one with the divine light.
Free to plumb the depths of hell
And unite with the divine darkness.
Free to be the flame it was meant to be.
Destroying, creating, blazing,
Being itself. Fire alive.
No longer fire in the shadows!

LOST FRIEND

I'll never see the house again.
The rain washed it away from my life
That bitter January morning
When the red gates shut behind me for the last time.
The rickshaw wheels beat time to my heart's sobs,
Suppressed behind formal goodbyes.
The cobra-lily tree waved its last farewell,
The slender '*amloki*' trees wept their leaves after me
As the little grey house vanished in the silver-mist rain.
Bougainvillea shadows dimmed my eyes as it passed from view.
And my guardians and friends … the cloud-dark mango trees
Whispered through the rain "Don't go!"
As I turned away and wept in my heart,
As I weep now!

I didn't want to go – they forced me!
I didn't want to leave, to say goodbye!
I'll never see my friends again!

I'll never smell the sweet, cold air
Or hear the night-time rush of birds' wings
Sweeping overhead in time to my dreams.
Never hear the squeak of pulley-wheels
Echoing around the old well,
Under the cloud of tamarind leaves,
As the dark water lips up in the bucket from the fragrant depths.
Never smell the tang of '*amloki*' flowers in bloom,
Or taste the brown tamarind fruit and the wrinkled '*kul*' …
essence of joy!
Never feel the honey-gold touch of the winter sun
Flowing down my back,
Or the rough warmth of the gravel-strewn path
Under my bare feet,
As I live through a magical world

Of flowers and trees and birds and dogs,
And become one with the light and air.
The '*bokul*' flowers star my path
And marigolds enamel my feet with gold.
The gardenia sprays my nights and days
With its magical perfume,
And the royal lemon-tree claims its rights to my senses!
The hoopoe raises its crest in astonishment
When I stand still for a minute,
But the heavy-bodied crow-pheasant
'Koob-koobs' its approval.
I feel the silken grass amidst my toes
And the swelling joy of knowing I belong
In this magical world of trees and leaves and grass and flowers
And the sweet-spice fragrance of unknown herbs.

And then I return to the world where I don't fit.
Where nights and days don't match
But blend together in a patchwork of duns and greys.
And I have no escape...
Only my mind gropes for the images of my lost world.
My lost friend!

WINTER IN SPRING

I think I'm in the Spring of my life,
My heart tells me so…
I watch Nature turn the Wheel of Seasons
And Winter is over.
Spring is in the doorway, with colours
And burgeoning warmth for Earth to revive.

Then I see the dry leaves of yesterday
Shaken by the dancing wind,
Drifting down…
To lie scattered on the growing grass,
To be absorbed into the earth
Or swept up by impatient hands
And flung onto the pyre of years.

The heaps of dead and yellow and brown grow larger.
Nature needs to shake away the detritus,
To make place for the fresh and green,
Young life to carry Life forward into a new year.

My eyes see …
My brain tells me …
Your Winter lives now in your Spring
And your year is almost over.

It's been a good year!

TRUE LOVE

Say what others may
About the ties of blood
And everything else about the love
Parents have for children
And children for parents
And grandmothers and grandfathers
- wrinkle cheeked and smiling -
Loving grandchildren with all their heart.
And brothers and sisters,
And lovers arm-in-arm
And husbands and wives,
Newly married or in their golden year,
And boyfriends and girlfriends,
And keeping faith and love ...
Say what you will,
There is no love greater than that between true friends.

That is love, real love,
That asks for nothing
Except maybe an occasional 'Hi!' and 'Hullo!'
And knows that nothing is required
Except to be a friend -
And know the joys and sorrows,
The pain and bliss
And be able to listen
And speak hot words
And love when you are being harsh.
Because she is your friend.
Your sweet-as-honey friend.
No, there is no greater love than that!

SOUL PAIN

Which is harder to bear.
The pain in your body
Or in your heart?
And do you really care
For any one of them
When there's a worse pain
Tearing you apart?
A pain in the darkest depths of you,
A pain no thought can cure
Or light can reach.
A pain that is embedded in what is you.
A pain that is the torment of your soul.
A voicelessness,
Shrieks that even you can't hear,
Which you can only feel.
Tears that drown you in their bitterness.
Drowning your body and mind
But not the depths of you.
For that one pain remains …
The torment of your soul.

EMBER-GLOW

The fire dies down,
The ember-glow remains.
Warming not just the hearth
But the room beyond
With memories of golden glow
And flashing sparkles.

In a little while the embers too
Will be turned to ash.
The wind will blow them away
To the corners of other memories.

Memories of other fires
Burning brightly now,
But soon to die down
To another ember-glow.

REPEAT

I saw you walk away from me
Into the shadow where I couldn't go.
I reached to take your hand
But you just smiled
And kissed me one last time.
I heard your whisper,
I saw you smile again
And look back once more,
Then step away from me,
And let the shadow draw you
Into its sheltering arms.
And you left me an empty shell –

To be filled again with light and joy?

TWO MONSOONS

Rain-slicked roads and streaming house-fronts,
Spattered windshields, wipers flicking futile fingers at the drops.
Sodden leaves patchwork the kerbs
As life slithers by in a steady stream under umbrellas dripping chill.
Splashes and sprays on reluctant feet,
And a mess of mud hurriedly sidestepped.
Dancers foxtrot with puddles and two-step with the rain.
Odoriferous earth, spiced with the pungency of decay,
Oily mud, household refuse soaked and mashed.
A sudden counterpoint of wet earth and leaves and grass
From some rare garden-patch
Send tingling memories hunting into the past,
Where another monsoon day lies hidden
In the accumulated dust of years and the covering cobwebs of age.

Rain-churned paths, a stream of red
Amidst the washed green-and-brown rows of *sal*,
Silver spears from grey-wool clouds
Hanging over the dark wet clouds of mango groves,
And the brush-straight coconut trees.
Leaf-patched roads, fragrantly wet, jigsawed by silver puddles
Where raindrop-fairies spring up, then vanish into memory.
Bare feet playing catch-as-catch-can
With the pools of silver wet that form and unform again
In the greenness of the meadows,
Where damp-skinned cows
Blow their hay-sweet breath at me.
And Kanu-goala's mother calls us in, out of the wet,
Into the warmth of an earth cup of fresh milk.

MAYA

There is no horizon,
No straight line pulling us straight to reach it
With temptations of light and glory.
The horizon isn't there ...

There is no sky
Showing us paintings of heaven
Pure and untainted and bathed in pearly light.
Heaven doesn't exist ...

There is no black hole that whispers of hell,
Dark and bathed in blazing fires.
There is no hell ...

There is only you
With your heaven and hell churning inside you.
And the horizon you have set for yourself.

WANT

They say that if you want something
And want it hard enough
Sooner or later you will get it.
Sooner, in fact.

In fact, you don't.
Your wanting never ends
Through the sun-spattered days
And dream-woven nights.

Through the long hours of idleness
When phantom wishes
Shade your thoughts with weary waiting
For that which you seek but never get.

Too, through the short eons of work,
When the clanging, busy hours
Beat time to the one refrain
In your brain
- I want it! I do!

But you never get it,
Never, though the longing for it
May lie like an ache
In the pit of your soul.

NATURE'S DANCE

The bird fluttered its wings
And the leaves fluttered too
In tune to its beat,
In a dance that's been going on forever.
It's a dance few can see
And fewer still can feel the music of that dance.
Nature created it in the womb of time,
And composed the music of its patterns.
She is creator and composer
And conductor of Her orchestra and dance.
The Universe hears it
And dances in time.

Only humans are the discord,
Breaking the rhythm,
Tearing into the delicate balanced steps
With clumsy superiority.

But Nature waits …
Waits till She knows it's time
To correct the rhythm, correct the steps
And bring back the pattern to what it should be.
And then …
Then we puny, good-for-nothing creations of Nature Herself …
We overstep the line
And are slapped down to dust.

TRAIN JOURNEY

Two fingers of steel
Pointing to a horizon I'll never reach.
They dip and rise,
Curve and straighten
And curve again.
Still pointing …
Rustling walls of green rise up,
And drop away.
Then greening waves take over,
Rolling to the horizon,
Fenced with wires and shafts
Like fingers pointing to the sky.
Sunshine gleams with tender fury
From a blue that goes streaming by.
Rain pours down
From sagging wombs of clouds,
Rippling spears of silver
Impale the brown and green earth.
Shadows chase across the lines
That race unendingly ahead.
My eyes follow,
Trying to probe the horizon I'll never reach.

TIME TO ME

Give me some time to think for myself,
Give me some time to see what *I* see,
Give me some time to stand up straight,
Give me time to be me!

Give me some time to set my goal,
Give me some time to find a way,
Give me some time to think out loud,
Give me time for *my* day!

Don't set me walls that I can't climb,
Don't give me sums that heat my head,
Don't tell me 'yes' when I want 'no',
Don't show me where to tread!

I'll rage against a world that's false,
I'll slam my fists against ugly words.
I'll cry out loud, though I can't speak,
I'll fight to find my sword.

Let me take Time and make it my own,
Let me mould the light so I can see,
Let me draw the darkness about myself
And see the depths that can be me.

WRITER'S WOE

The blank canvas you have …
It's all hunky-dory when you think of it.
You picture the words you'll write
And the lines you'll sketch.
You see the stories you want the world to hear
And the paintings you want them to see.

But when you hold it in your hand
And pick up your pen
Then what have you got?
Just a wild race of thoughts.
Uncontrolled, untamed,
Trying to form into words.
Writhing across your mind,
Then spilling over onto the blank sheet
And racing away in an unbridled gallop
While the reins of control
Turn into imaginary puffs of the mind.

And suddenly, all is still again
Calm and gentle,
At peace with the war waged.
Then you see the golden lines
Etched across the blank sheet,
Lines your heart has drawn …
More beautiful than anything your mind could imagine.

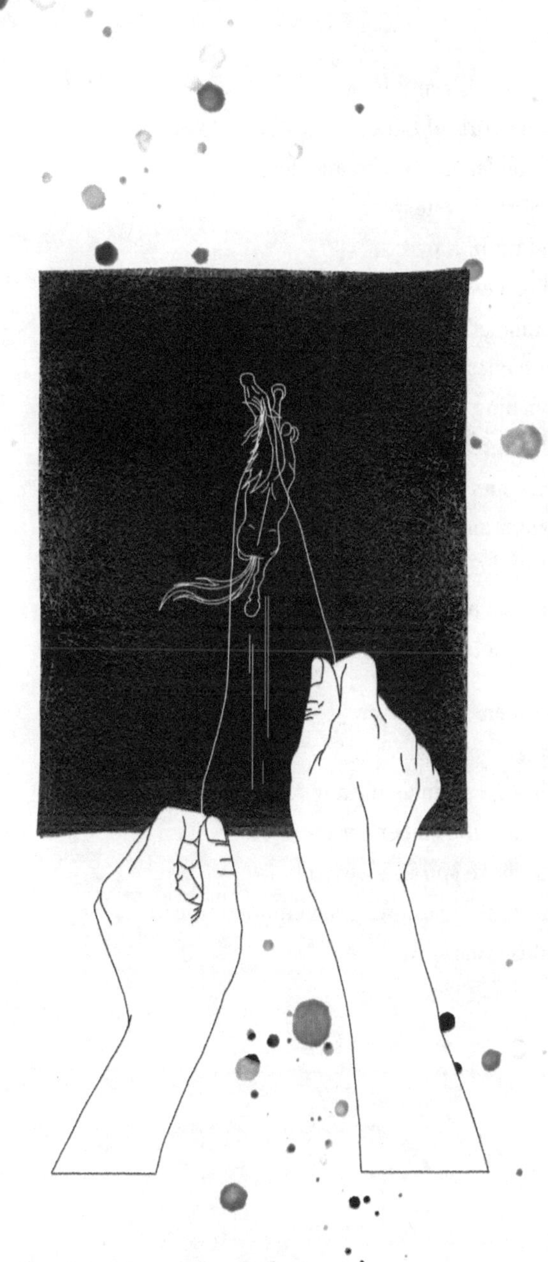

A BURNING

Dry branches and twigs,
Peeling curls of bark,
Drifting leaves, brown and sere,
Detritus of yesteryear
Piled up in a pyre
To burn away the useless
And make way for the young and new.
The flames soar up …
A burning crown to place on the head of those to come.
A drifting breeze scatter the last oblations
As colours are flung on the gold.
Warmth and light spread and summons Life
Out of the old earth and air –
To dance again with the sparks
And graceful spire of light.

And then … it's over.
A final look back,
Perhaps a sprinkle of rain
To douse the embers of the past.
The smoke spirals slowly up,
The scent of yesterday's memories spreads …
And is gone.

QUESTIONS

There comes a point when questions can't be asked
Or answered any more.
When you can't ask … or reply …
Or even want to!
When 'Why?' or 'What?' or 'Where?' or 'How?'
Have no meaning left for anyone but you.

You don't want to face the world
And see others point at them,
Chew them up and spit them back in your face.
Or trample them with their muddy minds,
And burn with their so-called opinions.

They're *your* questions
And matter little to anybody else.

PICTURE MEMORY

Resting my mind in the wells of thought
I walk the cool dimness of pine-woods shaded by dreams.
Hear the rippling music of sweet waters
Trickling over ferns and pebbles, musky with enchantment.
Feel velvet moss, like the palms of baby hands,
Catch the boles of trees I sketch with my memories.
Shaded secret paths, grass-grown and unmarked,
Untrodden by experience, uncrushed by knowledge,
Running through shades of thought like rivulets of light.
Through my thoughts sing the sweet tunes
Of a jungle-hidden bird, secret and soft,
Nesting in the branches of my dream trees
Where life blooms anew in waxy green candles
That promise light and life.
The sound of rushing waters and dancing winds
Whisper a song of contentment.
And I tread again, in my dream of innocence,
The road I know and love …
That ends in the waiting arms of Knowledge.
They embrace me like the sun,
And I am cinder-burnt.
My thoughts, my dreams struggle to return
To the arms of the shadow-trees
And the velvet-soft caresses of moss and breeze.
But I stumble on the smooth stone road that Knowledge built,
Where greens and greys are transformed
To jewel-bright hardness.
The whispered songs of innocence fade away
And I am in the sunlight …
In the full glare of Knowing!

CONFECTIONARY

Sunset …
The sun embedded in whipped cream decoration of clouds,
A lavish ladleful of golden syrup poured over the sky
Trickling downwards to the leaves of the trees,
And the house-tops catch a few drops
And savour it slowly,
Reluctant to pass it down
To the plum-sauce-shadow-wrapped bushes
Garnished with a scatter of nut-gold sunlight scraps.
A soft dash of cinnamon-powder-brown tree-trunk shades
That spread with slow mistiness
Over the whole confection,
As the spoon of night dips with greedy glee,
And the plum-sauce swirls up with the cinnamon.
Honey and nuts and cream melt together
Till the bowl of night is empty
And ready again for another delicious confection.

MUSIC

Music that crushes you down
And breaks your soul,
Then lifts you up and makes you whole.
It finds the gaps in walls you've built
To protect yourself from the world.
It touches the armour you wear
To hide your heart,
And strokes it with disarming tenderness
Till it's pliant and soft as a baby bird
Cradled in your hand.

And when your heart and mind
And body and soul have melted,
Then the soaring crescendo
Whirls away the curtains
Of doubt and fear and despair,
And smashes you - heart and soul,
With its hammer of harmony
And rebuilds you from the crumbled bits
And makes you real.

WHY AM I ?

Why am I what I am?
A confused bundle of shrinking desires
Looking for an outlet,
And finding one at last, cringing back in fright!
A mass of raving dreams to mend the world and all in it
And … most important … myself.
Values clung to with shaking hands,
Worried eyes seeing what they don't want to see,
And ears catching sounds the brain blocks out!

Everything I am … I am not!
For I have modelled myself again,
Taking that divine clay of which It made me
Pinching and battering myself into an alien shape -
Giving it the varnish of everyone else's approval,
And, in the process, losing the Me in me.

And then I question myself in frightened whispers
Knowing the answer, scared to ask,
Yet asking again … and again …
Why? Why am I just what I am?

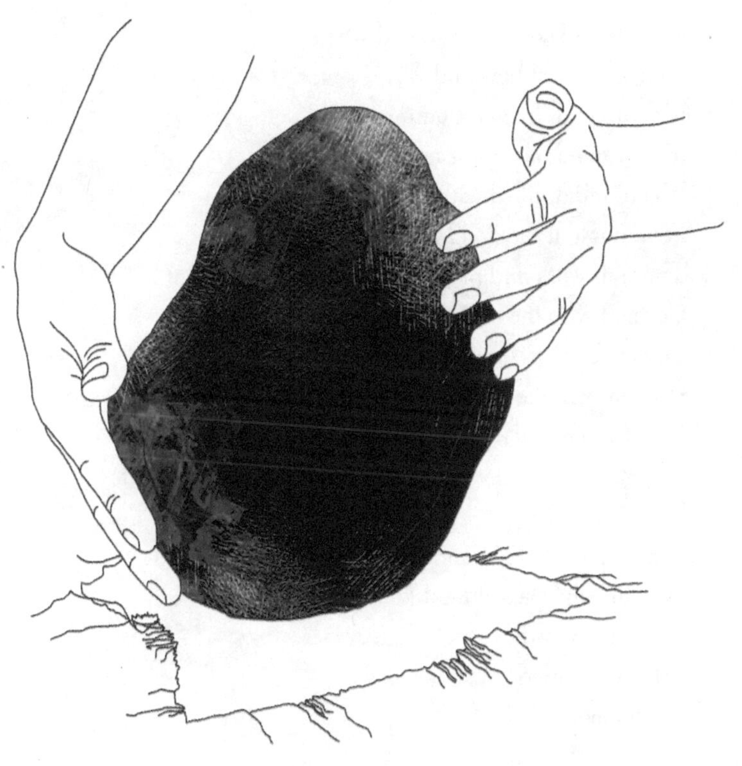

MIND

I saw my mind in a clear glass,
Sunlit, with the light of *me* about it.
I saw each facet, diamond-bright,
Without the stain of doubt or fear,
Brilliant in knowing what and where
And when and how and why.
It's *my* mind, free and untrammelled,
It's *my* mind, cloudless as autumn skies.
It's *my* mind, filled with my heartbeat,
Pounding out the holiday rhythm
Through work and play and the louds and softs of life.
Covered with the mist-soft whiteness
Of new blossoms, tender as the dawn.
Painted with the pure colours of evening
Reeling across the skies and drawing behind it
The star-spattered veil of night.
My mind –
The essence of light and shade and dark and bright
And the highs and lows I know and am happy with.
It is me, my own!
I claim my mind -
I claim me.

TONGUE TIED

Stop that noise, say my ears
And my tongue laughs in glee,
For decibels are precious as gems
On that sinuous ultimate in weaponry.
So small, so soft … and yet
With uncontrolled power to batter my poor ears
… pathetic guardians to my thoughts …
And they face one onslaught after another.

And then it is still.

But even in its stillness it's the holocaust-causer.
Yes, even in its ominous silence
Its sound strikes again and again
In the coiling recesses of the brain.
And that form - asleep - is more terrible
Than when awake.
For nothing stops the clamour of that guerrilla tongue,
When the dread 'No noise'
Is so much more terrible and powerful
Than any sound heard.
For there is nothing worse
Than to hear the un-said.

A PLEA FOR SLEEP

Owl, don't screech,
But let my sleep come soft-footed,
Wreathed with garbled dreams
Weaving fantasies in my day-weary mind.
Let my eyelids rest on my eyes at last,
And forget awhile tomorrow's task
Of being guardsmen to my informers.
Let my head hunt for something soft …
Softer to balance it than my seething spine.
And let the spate of life ebb softly back a little way,
To let gentling sleep come at last
With outstretched arms
And gather my day-ravaged body and blistered brain
Into its tender keeping for a little while.
Until the light snatches me back again
From those gentle hands.
So, owl, don't screech!

FUTILITY

Futility is a word I never knew
Till I met you.
You changed the way I lived and loved
And knew the world with joyful innocence.

I know the world with eyes of age
And reluctant wisdom
Learnt on the anvil of your love.

I live for you, your love, your self,
And negate myself … futile in my life!

A new word - Futility -
Is added to the vocabulary of my life.
A word I never knew till I met you.

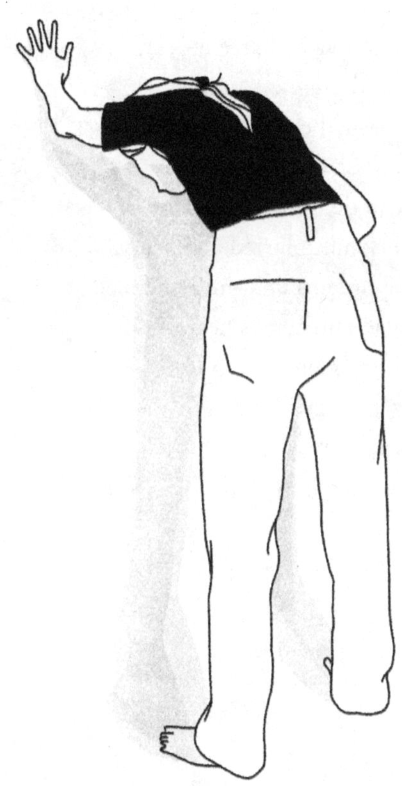

FIRST RAIN IN JABALPUR

Gentle rain on the sun-burnt face of the earth
And the soft shadows of clouds
Grazing across the sky like herds of elephants,
Wash the browns with the cool shimmer of greys.
A sweep of silver, a touch of greeny-gray,
And dust lies tamed, fragrant and rich.
Rocks blacken, washed clean of bleaching dust.
A whisper of life runs through the grass ...
White and tense in the glare of summer ...
As the wet wool clouds, blurred and heavy,
Lowers the silver curtains that shifts and melts
And wipes away the breathless heat.
Coolness sensed, then felt,
Savoured slowly in every fibre
And through every pore.
Thirst quenched at last!

SEARCHING A PATH

Scared of existing as I am,
I'm lost in the planned maze of my life,
Hunting frantically for a way that'll take me out.
Not out of Life,
Not to Death,
Oh no, that would be too complete ...
But to a source of fulfilment,
That ever-growing space of Light and delicate shades.
Fulfilment that will let me see me as myself -
Completed!

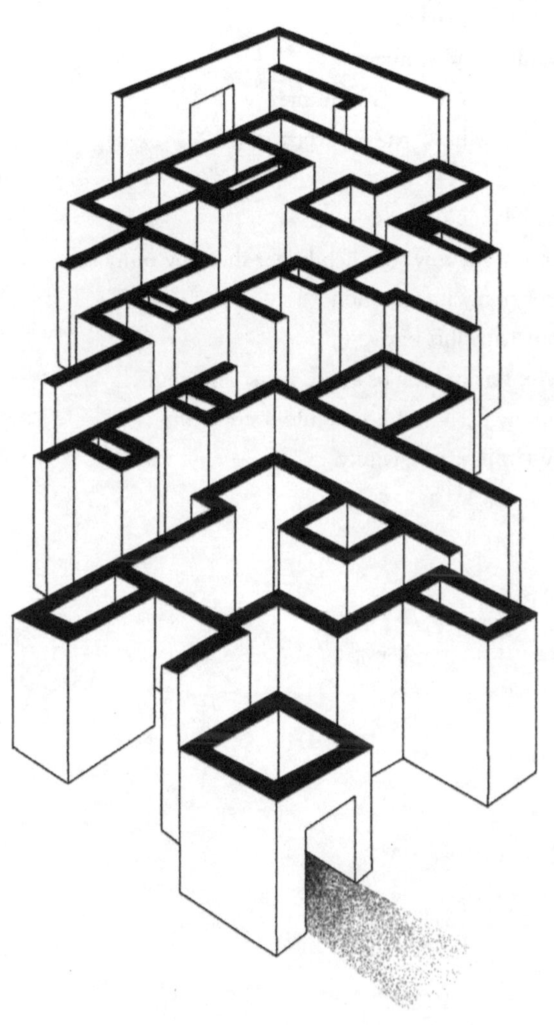

MY SHADOW ME

By what strange whim
Did Nature, my Mother,
Make my shadow larger than me?
Did she know how true a parody of me
That would be?
Did she joke on purpose,
Making my shadow so much larger than my puny self.
A mirror of my imagination
That outstrips this body,
This Me, this bundle of mind, heart and soul …
Turning my flesh and bones into a nonentity …
But my Brain into Divinity.

BREAK AND MAKE

If the sun didn't set
How would you know there's a day?
If the storm didn't rage
And crush your flowers
You wouldn't have known about fragrance.
If your heart didn't break
You wouldn't have found your soul.

HERMIT-CRAB

Be a hermit-crab in this world of noise
And uncaring hearts and minds.
Build your shell with your resources
And retreat into it.
Shut the door on a world that doesn't want you to be you.
Turn your back on unwanted thoughts storming your mind,
Blowing in the pollution that chokes you.

Just retreat into a world that knows you,
That you have created for yourself.
That's not being a coward,
That's not being negative!
That is being you in a world *you* made,
Like some lonely hermit-crab on the ocean floor.
Lonely amidst so much life and movement and sound,
Always carrying its own home, its world.

Be a hermit-crab …
Because you don't fit anymore,
Because you question the cement-set world,
And you're not welcome in this world of other people.

UGLY MURDER

I'm so sorry I killed you.
Smashed you down till you were nothing but a gray splodge.
I didn't see your beauty …
The eight graceful legs moving like a dancer's
As you leapt from one spot to another.
Those gleaming eyes that saw everything …
Even the least scrap of life that could be food.
But they didn't see that merciless slipper
That ended your life.
I'm so sorry.

I'm so sorry I killed you.
Sprayed you with a cloud of poison that left you inert,
Life ebbing away in terrible convulsions.
I didn't see your beauty …
The gleaming agate-brown body
Sliding smoothly through light and shade.
The butter-yellow head
Sensing sustenance in the darkest corners.
And the sudden lift of shimmer-bright wings
Swishing away from danger.
But it couldn't escape that cloud of death I unleashed.
I'm so sorry.

I'm so sorry I killed you.
Swept you down a noisome drain with acid water,
And all you could do was writhe in agony
As the pain burned through your body.
I didn't see your beauty …

Didn't see the sinuously graceful movements
Or the blur of a hundred legs
Moving like a tasselled fringe in a spring breeze,
Sliding you through paper-thin cracks
As you sought for shelter.
But they couldn't shelter you from the burning liquid I poured.
I'm so sorry.

Why did I kill you?
Why didn't I kill the butterfly that startlingly settled on my head?
I just squealed, half-laughing,
And shook it away.
Why didn't I kill the burring bumble-bee,
It's drone vibrating the air as it flew in and out.
Or the grass-green dragonfly, shimmering it's glassy wings in the sun.

Were these too beautiful to kill?
Do I kill only the ugly?

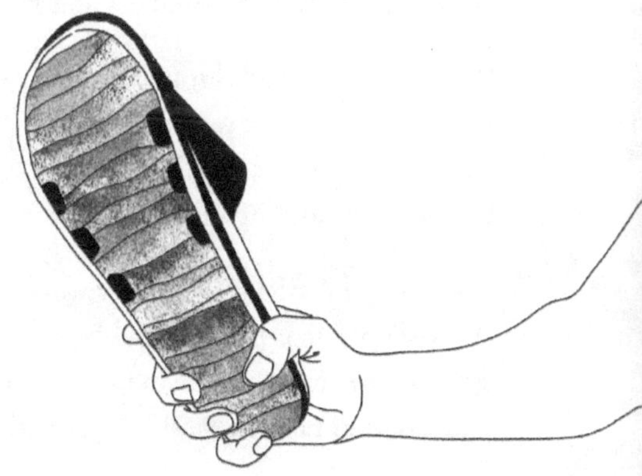

(with apologies to my kids, whose unanimous reaction to this was 'Eeeeksss!)

RHYMES TO LOVE AND HATE

If I had time to write a letter
To love and hate, or neutral or worse.
I think I could do it … but wouldn't it be better
To pen a few lines of doggerel verse?

Verses of hate to what we call Love,
And then of love to that opposite thing.
Maybe it'll fit like the proverbial glove
And give our thoughts a pendulum swing.

So here I go, with faltering pen,
To pen the verses demanded of me.
Hear me out, my friends … and then …
Of the right or wrong the judge you'll be!

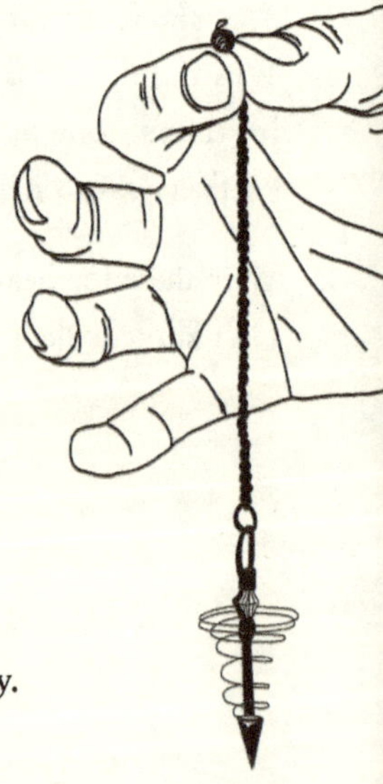

I start with hate for gentle Love.
Dear Love, for you these rhymes I write.
You're always known as a gift from above,
A bringer of joy and sweetness and light.

We dream of you all through our life,
At every step of our weary way.
The love of parents, of kids, of wife,
Of husbands and friends and companions gay.

But Love, the gifts you cast our way
Are balloons that pop and bubbles that burst.
They're dreams that fade at break of day,
Leaving chill and fear and hunger and thirst!

So Love, my dear, stay away from me,
For I don't believe the tales I hear
Of your beauty and grace and purity …
Hah!
I only feel your pain and fear!

And now, Dear Hate, painted so black
And loathed and feared in equal measure.
Here are some rhymes of love from me …
For sadly, no-one sees that you're a true treasure.

We try to avoid you and piously raise
Our eyes to Heaven and say you're bad.
We shun you ever, and Love we praise,
And if you leave, we say we're glad.

But nobody sees the true nature of you,
The cleansing fire you bring to our life.
The feelings you bring are real and true,
And clear a path through the swamp of strife.

Our minds, when clogged with social norms
And fogged by thoughts that others may bring,
Is cleared by you in all your forms …
Our thoughts are free to soar and sing.

Hate, my dear, you're the finger that points
To our true nature and depths of our soul.
You show us all our cracks and joints
So we can repair them and then be whole.

And so I dare to write these rhymes,
Of love for Hate and hate for Love.
But I admit, my friends, it's always better
When Love and Hate fit like a glove!

SUNLIGHT DREAMS

I'll sit in the sunlight
And maybe dream of the life I haven't lived,
But wanted to live.
And talk to the people I haven't met
But should have known.
I'll see those places I could have seen,
Beautiful in my dreams.
I'll sing those songs I wanted to sing
But didn't find the tune in me.
And dance on the wind, light as air,
Which I couldn't on clumsy feet.
I'll dream in the sunlight
Of the Me I wanted to be.

THE DARE

My life isn't yours to trample and mould
And cover in the mud of your dark thoughts.
It isn't yours to toss about carelessly
Like an old football, worn out with use
And constant kickings of schoolboy-harsh feet.
It isn't your life to hold and crush
And sneer and jibe and breathe the curses
Your mind nurtures, to destroy my life
With the dark purgings of your thoughts,
Unwanted pictures of your soul.

My life is mine, bright with my light,
Coloured with the thoughts given to me
By my own Nature.
Formed from the beauty seen with my eyes
And the awe of heaven and hell
That fills my heart.
It is mine
And I dare you to try and take an atom from me!

A PRAYER

I bow to you,
Prakriti!
Force encompassing all forces
In the mighty Allness of you!
You are Everything and Everyone!
Man can sing your anthem,
But his puny mind … which You have let him call great,
Can't encompass one Heartbeat of you.
Can't feel within his life-flow Your Flow!
You nestle within him and he in You.
His thoughts are Yours, his mind is You!
His pulse beats in You,
You, who are the pulse of the Universe.
Mother, Father,
Creator, Keeper, Destroyer.
Energy …
Timeless Time.
Prakriti!

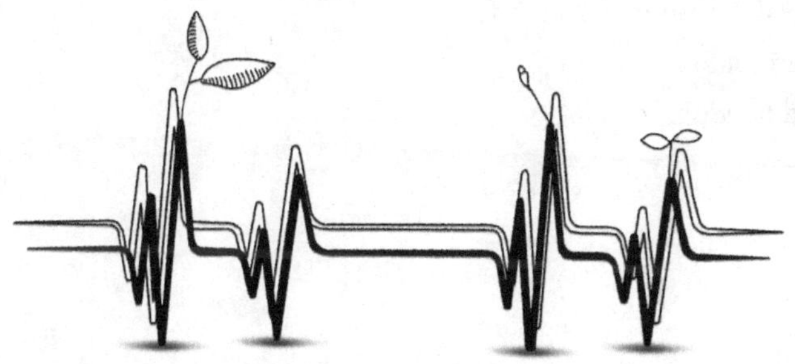

I SEARCH

I search for freedom …

And find it in the dancing dust-motes
In the beam of light
That enters my mind through the one window I have left open.

I find it in the dew-drops on the leaf-tips,
Glittering like diamonds
In the tender rays of the morning sun that I let in through my heart.

I find it in the gust of fragrant wind
That enters through the chink in the shutters of my mind
And drives away the mustiness of ages.

I find it in the single flower
Fallen on the ground like a lost gem
That catches my jaded eyes with its coloured gleam.

I find it in the whisper of a song
Half-heard, half-felt
That I allow to enter my head through my reluctant ears.

I find the freedom I search for
All around me.
I find freedom in me.

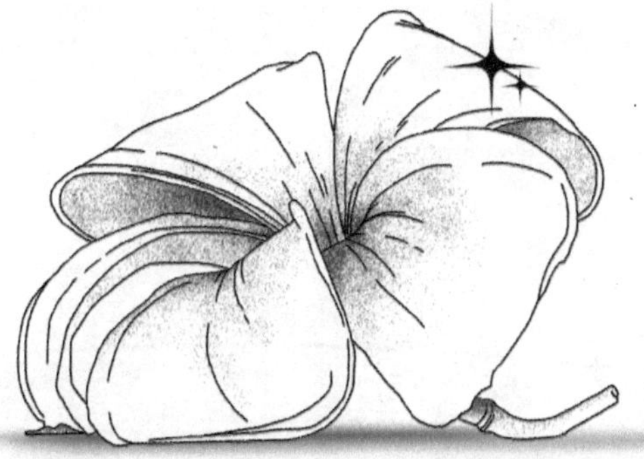

THE GOLDEN THREAD

There is a golden thread that guides my mind,
Leading it through this maze of Life.
Not to the bull-shouldered monster within …
It leads me out … it holds my hand,
And, like a trusting child, I follow it.
For I know, with my untethered instinct,
That it'll lead me where I want to go,
To the goal I really want to reach,
The goal I need.
For it's the breath of my breath,
My essence.
I know I can hold that thread
And go where I want to - not where I have to!
I know that my bliss waits for me
At the end of my golden thread of Hope.

I know I can reach it, but …
Do I trust myself to grasp it?

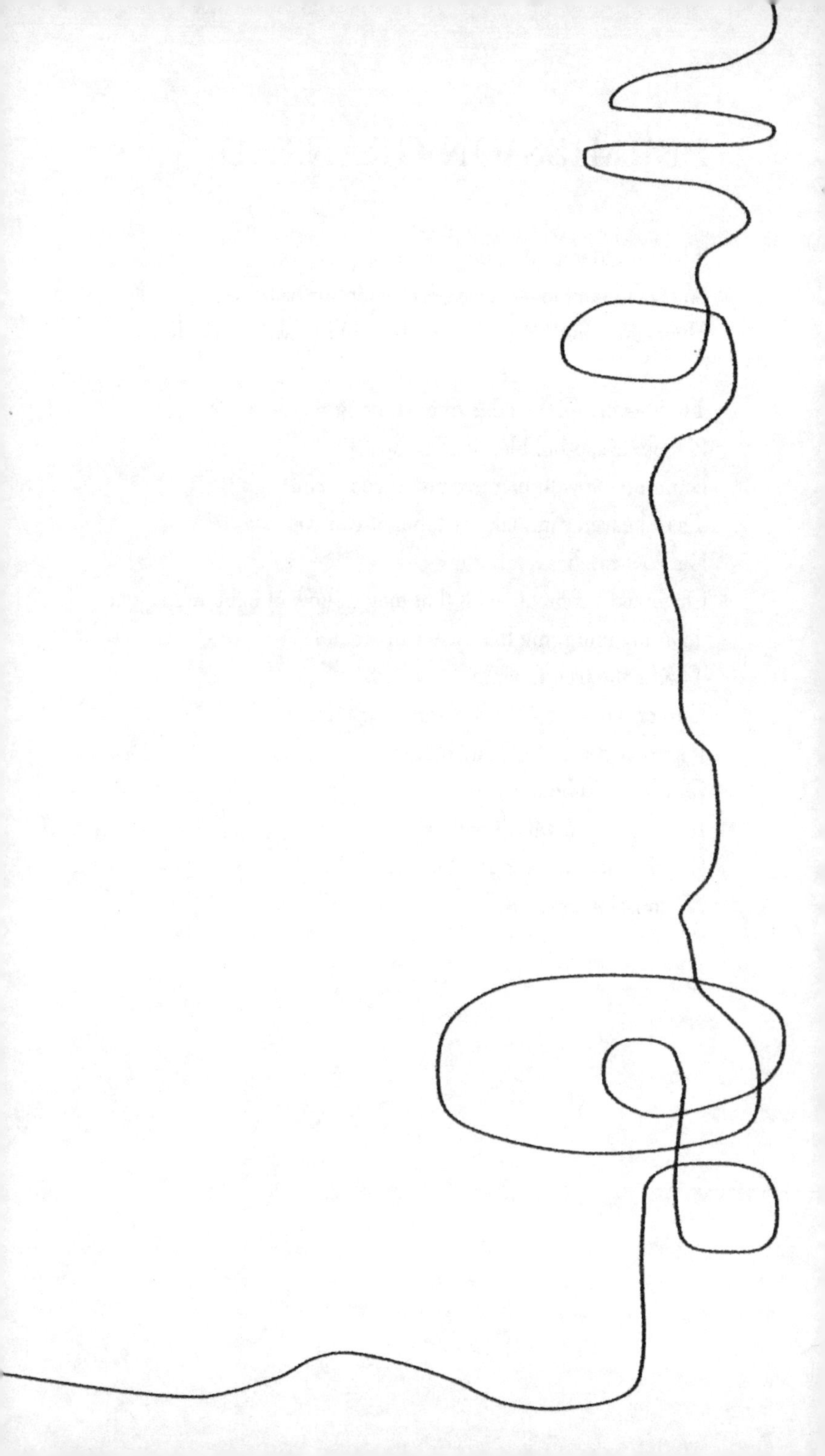

PERMISSION GRANTED

'Hold on to your dreams', you say,
And magnanimously give permission for heartbreak.
How can I hold on to that golden bubble with work-clumsy fingers
That hovers on the edge of destroying the dreams?
It's my dream-bubble, floating up
Blinding me with pictures more wonderful
Than heaven can make or thought can concoct.
For how can heaven bestow,
Or thought compete with that magic show of light and colour
That my mind, my Essence, can create!
That is the true Divinity
Ensconced within, even before I was imagined.
It's not a child's birthday balloon
Or a soap-bubble toy.
It's what I am, what I will be forever.
So who gave you the right to say
"Permission granted!"

TRUE FRIENDSHIP

What does true friendship do?
It grabs you with both hands
When you need it most,
To mend your broken heart
Or your tattered dreams.
It catches the wisp of your fading hope
With gentle fingers
And stuffs it back into the empty shell you have become.
It lights the guttering candle in your eyes
So you can see the world renewed.
It melts the ice in your soul
So the river of your being can flow again.

True friendship isn't something to be bought by cheap cards
And gimcrack gifts,
And inane sayings.

It's the essence of existence, of true love.

CHANGE

Don't ask me to change,
My change lies in me …

In my eyes
That open every day to see the world again.
In my skin
That feels the tender touch of sun and wind and rain.
In my hands
That lifts the burdens grown heavy yesterday.
In my feet
That walks that extra mile I thought I couldn't.
In my heart
That feels again the thumping beat of the universe.
In my head
That moulds again worlds within worlds.

Don't ask me to change
I *am* the change.

PRAYER TO ME

Joy in the morning
When I know I'm awake
And see the light,
Feel the breeze on my cheeks
And smell life.
Joy in the morning flows from Me.

Joy in the afternoon
When the day-time clangour
Assaults my ears
And tells me that I live.
Joy in the afternoon flows from Me.

Joy in the evening
When the hours wind down
And I find comfort
In the warmth of home
Where life rests.
Joy in the evening flows from Me.

Joy at night
When the star-spattered darkness
Covers me with comfort
And dreams cradle me
In my bed of life.
Joy at night flows from Me.

www.ingramcontent.com/pod-product-compliance
Lightning Source LLC
La Vergne TN
LVHW091039150826
845672LV00006BA/1887

* 9 7 9 8 8 9 5 4 4 2 9 6 8 *